MAGICAL DESERT

.

MAGICAL DESERT

HELENA WEISS-MEYER

CREATIVE ARTS BOOK COMPANY
Berkeley • California 1999

Translated by Margaret Crosland
and the author, 1997

Cover design by Helena Weiss-Meyer

The Seven Spiritual Laws of Success
used with permission of author

For information contact:
Creative Arts Book Company
833 Bancroft Way
Berkeley, California 94710

ISBN 0-88739-169-9
Library of Congress Catalog Number 97-68998

Printed in the United States of America

To the two Mélanies found again ...

To my Petite-Fleur...

To my Raïssa...

"We are the heavens, we are the earth, in the end we cease to live and feel, we love each other in the world beyond...
I offer you eternity, take hold of it."

Paul Verlaine

MAGICAL DESERT

MAGICAL DESERT

I should like to please or displease in a single line,
but, most of all, not to cause indifference.
I should like to touch, disturb, upset over-rigid
minds, and restore some emotional order to an
utterly troubled world.
I should like to make the heart speak wildly with
no restraint whatever.

"A story extra-ordinary."
A tale of naked truth.

Love at first sight,
A meeting, a beautiful story.

My life stopped and everything began again.
The moments of silence, the waiting, the pain,
the plunge into eternity.

Do you lack for spontaneity to search more
deeply, to be more certain of the unbreakable
links that sustain me?
Have you tried to retreat within yourself to
understand the attractions and profound
motivations of your heart?
In secrecy?
In times of meditation?

My only weapons are the Love and patience
I bear you.

In a letter, I ask you to make a decision to end
our story, if that is what you want.
It is very painful to know nothing.
I don't understand.
No answers.
Then, after much trouble, we speak by telephone:
      "Don't think about me, just listen to my
music; it's for you."
Love in silence.
Total romance.
And here begins a loving search that will never end.

I hope I shan't crack up.
I hope I shan't worry my friend,
confidant and spiritual sister,
always there for me,
if only by listening in silence.

Until now I had little need of outside help.
If I suddenly felt depressed, I looked within myself
quietly, and all my sorrow faded away.
I feel I shan't emerge from this alone.
I'm afraid of needing someone's presence
all the time.

I hear my demons scoffing at me:

"You see, Helena, you thought you could fly
higher than me. You thought that Love
protected you from everything.
Not so, I was truly here.
I didn't consume you slowly, I was waiting
until you were ready to
eat, then I could devour you in one
mouthful.
I shall have to try again and take several
mouthfuls, for you're tough,
but it's only a question of time.
Your strength, your Love belonged to the
imagination, but your solitude was truly
real.

And don't think that Paul will help you.

He can't, even though he'd like to, simply
because he's never shared anything with you.
You were his muse for a moment, but muses
don't exist.
They allow artists to fantasize, to create,
to establish a link with the other world,
and to be inspired, that's all.
To live out a dream, all people and
backgrounds must be fictional.
You chose an extraordinary human creature.
Everything had to crash.
You knew it from the first second."

Yes, I knew it and I made the choice.

Years of imaginary happiness which filled me
with joy.
Years of searching within myself
brought me constant enrichment.
Paul was the one who revealed so much that was
buried within me.
Everything was there in a latent state.
Everything broke loose.
I have done no more than move a little further
forward each day.
One second of doubt, one second of fear and
I would find the solution;
I would find the response;
I would find relief.
It was all obvious, natural.

And it was natural for me to think it was due to
Paul, at least to my Love for Paul.
I still think so.

I for him, he for me, to achieve just one being,
that alchemist's fusion, that eternal flame, one
within the other, one for the other, thrilling to
the same harmony, to be in Love, to make Love.

It's so wretched to exist just for oneself alone.

Sometimes I try to put my theory to the test to
prove to myself that I've been merely a happy fool,
blinded by something that was only a myth, a few
notes of music on a spring day.
But it's all in vain.
Imperturbably the heart emerges victorious.
It's not obstinacy.
It's something else.

Difficult to describe those deep convictions
I carry within me that appeal not to my mind
but to my heart and also my flesh.
As though all the cells of my body quivered and
transmitted certainties to me;
certainties I was never mistaken about, because,
in fact they sprang from a memory that had no
place in my brain and the experience I gathered
as Helena.
My instinct and my intuition always work well for
me.
They know what is right.
I often force myself to appeal to reason and act
against my wishes.
As a rule the result is disastrous.
Allowing my heart to speak does not stop me
from being lucid.
On the contrary.

On several occasions I noticed, while speaking of
my destiny, Paul reacted violently,
as if I had spoken to him of his destiny.
I was indeed touching a tender spot.
It was not I who thought my destiny was
automatically his, it was he.
He seemed to be mingling together fatality, destiny
and spirituality; rejecting everything at once.

I am like the hidden side
which must not be evoked.
It's frustrating for a girl like me who wants to tell
what she knows.

I often have the impression our Love is something
that has been settled.

That's the way it is, nothing can be done about it;
that Love is sealed within the memory of the world.

Whatever we do, or whatever we say, our bond is
eternal and we must live with it.

No doubt this was the reason for our meeting.

No matter verbal or physical, no break can ever
exist.

And surely that is where lie the real, the beautiful,
and the true.

If the apparent reality is a break, the true reality is
an eternal Love that can never die;

it has never been born.

It is.

My eyes see this, my thoughts say this, but my
heart feels the contrary.
Can this lead to madness or to the impossibility
of defining things; to the limit of the imaginary
and the real, to nothingness,
there where everything is possible,
where knowledge is universal?
Do I possess a fragment of truth or am I
fantasizing in order to live through this harsh
reality while waiting for something better?
Intuitive truth or purely self-protective reaction?
Find out.

Today is Easter Sunday.

Several years ago, on this very day, I encountered a
being who was to turn my life upside down.
Years of waiting, patience, and deep solitude, accompanied
with sadness and also gleams of joy and ecstasy,
led me directly into a paradise of
purity and light.
It's easy to think that Paul is the man of my life.
But who can believe that I am the woman of his life?
Who, apart from myself and a few psychics whom I
manipulate perhaps rather easily, for my
concentration on this beloved being is so great.
I continue to hope, hope fills my existence utterly,
and I'm convinced this intense activity will one day
produce marvelous fruit.

I'm damnably in Love or else fit for the madhouse.
I must exorcise you from my being
or let you take root more deeply within me.
I think I have chosen to love you until
the end of my road.
If you knew how happy I am even if my burden is
sometimes heavy to bear.
I'm happy and radiant simply because I love you.
I think I could tolerate anything at this moment.
I began to be truly alive the day I met you.
Each day a little calmer, convinced that the way
I was taking was right.
I've learned so much, loving you in solitude.
I've learned how to wish for your happiness
before my own and suffer your unhappiness
as though it were mine.

I can't stop myself from thinking that if such
deep-seated things work within me through you,
it's not the same for you.
The famous law of action and reaction.
What do you do with all the thought-waves
I send you?
You have encased yourself in armor,
so they must be mounting up around you.
If they cannot reach your heart directly
they can surround and protect you.
Will those waves one day succeed in
piercing your armor like a laser?
You would be struck down by Love.

I believe in our Love immediately.
You fought against our Love.

I wanted to break things off officially with a letter.
But if the break had been declared, how would
that have changed things for me after all?
Absolutely nothing, apart from a few further
sorrows giving me the chance to love you better
still or to sink into a sickly state of devotion.
Am I responding to an infallible truth,
am I consciously taking refuge in an illusion in
order to withstand the shock?
So many things are that strong within me.

Is the feeling I'll never stop loving you temporary?
Is my vow of natural celibacy temporary too,
the vow I took without the slightest frustration,
should you not come back to me?
If I'm sometimes a little afraid of keeping my
promise until I die, it's only because my end
seems a long way away.
Is the absolute purity of these feelings
the fruit of my over-active imagination,
a hand-embroidered aspect of illusion?
I'm so happy at having lived through all that and
finally reached this stage.
I'm so lucky, for I'm fulfilling my dearest wish.
The torments matter little,
I'm living out my dreams.
Might you be merely a step in my life

before apotheosis?
Life can be so marvelous or cruel through the
strokes of destiny, but the exaggerated romanticism
that haunts me, always carries me away
to the fringes of the fantastic.

I've given up trying to forget you, for whatever I do,
everyday, life brings me back to you.
Although your music is not often broadcast on the
air, by chance something always intervenes at the
moment when I decide not to concentrate on you
anymore.
If I avoid you, if I blot you out, life brings you back
to me.
Life doesn't want me to break the contact and I
must try whatever happens to remain in harmony

with the rhythm of life.

I've made up my mind.

I no longer weep, I no longer complain.

If it's your wish to be free of me, I'm setting you free.

One worry less for you who have many others.

I was living a Love story in solitude, so it's hardly

surprising that our parting is in solitude as well.

There's a certain logic in all that.

Yet I should have liked you to show some pity

for my fate.

Have you ever shown compassion for a being

other than yourself?

Is it sensible for me to cling more and more closely?
My letter was intended to be decisive,
but once again I know nothing.
If at least you agreed, you would also have known
where you were, we would have made progress.
So don't you have any touch of heart?
Has it never occurred to you to put yourself
in my place, if only for a moment?
You must be unkind and selfish.
Why did I have to go through this?
To avoid being trapped by music or words.
To learn, perhaps, that when an artist is in the grip
of inspiration he's a sensitive being; the rest of the
time he's fighting his problematic ego and can't
give anything to others:
"I am a musician, I suffer."

Why does beauty suddenly turn ugly
as soon as it touches human reality?
Duality seems to be inscribed in men
since the beginning of time.

My states of mind change as the hours pass.
I feel better, I'm regaining my strength.
But yet again, I've decided not to try giving up
loving you any more.
I love you and it's the finest thing
that could happen to me.

Love has no laws, its extent is ever less clear.
Your schemes on its boundary leave me cold.
You and me forever or for a moment,
it matters little.
Intensity and sincerity matter, and Love, if only
expressed for a second, is eternal.
Why do I let myself go like this from time to time?
That letter, that accursed letter, and this waiting.
I must tell myself all the time,
things are the way they should be.
Solitude is good for me, I value it,
so what am I complaining about?
I need not worry about whether this situation
is temporary or not.
It exists and I'm living through it, that's all.
I'll see tomorrow what the morrow brings.

I mustn't rush things.
Silence is golden and I observe it well.
Is not perfect communion found in silence?
Now the sublime comes to the surface once more
and I delight in it.
I haven't reached this state only to fall back
to the slums of the earth.
Only I can bring back beauty into my life.
I must simply learn again and give myself time.

My only wish is that all should work out well for you.

Honestly, Helena, what do you expect from a
man who doesn't think about you, who leaves
you alone continually, giving no sign of life?
You're waiting for a miracle, a radical transfor-
mation, and a total change.
Is there the slightest visible sign to give you a
gleam of hope?
Not the slightest.
You know very well that if you were really the
woman of his life he wouldn't let you fret like this.
He would miss your presence,
he would need you in a small way.
And he'd have answered your letter quickly,
he couldn't have borne the idea of losing you.
Why?
Why is it hard for us to talk, to communicate?

I have the feeling you're a devil with an angel's face.
You are well aware of your own power.

There are no well-known explanations
for falling in Love.
The fact that we met and loved each other
was not due to chance.
But very rapidly, you checked your enthusiasm.
Fear no longer of mastering your feelings, of letting
yourself be carried away by the tide of emotions.
Create your music, if there is creation.
You can shape and reshape it as you wish.
But, you can't supervise Love,
you can only follow its flow and it shapes you as
it wishes.

Our Love is not the everyday kind.
In fact I'm more and more convinced that it is
beyond everything.
From the outside the gales and high tides are
visible, while the unchanging center is so beautiful,
so pure.
It's too bad that there are only two people in the
world who can understand.
It matters little if those beings
are called you and me.
Today, of course, I'm the only one who understands
and I build up the you-and-me existence with
myself alone.
Whatever happens,
if the future should separate us forever,
I shall have lived through this only with you.

However, if 'never' and 'always' are the most
delicate and uncertain words to use,
I firmly believe all I have said.
In fact these words are my prayers.
I can't be wrong for this is my soul speaking,
my deep-rooted truth, not my stubborn brain.
I should speak, in fact, of our deep-lying truth for
it's what we have in common;
it brought us together.
Our life together might seem reduced to nothing
but we share inner riches.
Often I succeed in making myself weep with joy.

It's odd, I almost became a researcher in
astrophysics.
The sky, the moon, the stars,
an everlasting spectacle of implacable, fascinating,
and enigmatic beauty.
Beauty, the universe, the infinite, all in one, one in
all; the infinitely beautiful, the infinitely grandiose,
the infinitely small.
The planet round the sun, the electron round the
nucleus, and the search going ever further.
Today I work on my body and soul.
All my results are positive.
If I think I'm going to meet failure,
I plod on persistently, I begin over and over again.
It matters little in what space-time one puts oneself.
Intangible Love supplies the answer.

The more I listen to your music,

the more I love it, the more I understand it.

The two of us together are total magic.

Desert-like, perhaps, but magical.

I think of you and all the blood in my body reaches

fever pitch.

Each cell in my body quivers

and tunes into your personal wavelength.

It's wonderful, it can't be expressed in words.

It is.

It's so simple, so easy to love.

Yet for some, it's full of complications:

Letting go, then moving always further, still higher.

Each time, however, one begins again.

One dismantles one's work, one re-makes it
a different way, and one tries to finish it
in order to surpass oneself unceasingly.

There is no end.
Everything is a perpetual beginning and ending.

This is surely the key to happiness:
Appreciate everything, including pain.
My life is rich; rich with you and rich through you.

I love you.

At first, over the years, I filled a notebook entitled
'*Hope or Love always*'. Then, as it was soon used
up, scraps of paper and pads of all sizes took over.
Now, I'm trying to put a little order
into my writing.
There can be no logical continuity in committing
states of soul to paper. It's good for me, however,
to trace my progress which is logical and evident.
The only way to reach this man is to wait for him
like Penelope and write to him.
If I stop, he won't be able to catch up.
I continue tirelessly.
Each thought turns toward you
at the risk of displeasing you.
The stake is chivalrous.
I am chivalrous.

Maybe I'm writing this book as a work of atonement,
inducing calm, bringing an end to the madness of
Love which inhibits body and soul.

Nevertheless, I don't want to stop loving you.
It's my greatest happiness, my greatest strength,
and a perpetual enrichment of my inner self.

*I will wait patiently, dreaming of the day when all of
our Love will come together and marry.*

I've always seen reincarnation as a phenomenon as
natural as the mere fact of breathing.
As a little girl I believed in ghosts
and the world beyond.
As an adolescent I studied physics solely to
encounter the realm of waves.
The concept of spirit-matter, which outstrips the
purely intellectual concept, was my first religion if
one can use such a term.
In the universe, all is a wave and all matter on
earth, human beings included,
come from the stars.
Is the word 'cosmetic', relating to beauty,
not derived from 'cosmos',
the beauty of human beings passing through space?
Don't the most ancient mythologies and beliefs

coincide magnificently with the most elaborate
and sophisticated scientific research?
There is no mystery about that.
It's a logical continuation of the human spirit.
One has only to take the necessary time
to go to the root of things.

My story, so beautiful and difficult,
must have reached the far past.
You were a musician and you played the
forerunner of the harpsichord.
You were my music teacher.
I lived in a castle in Scotland.
We were both very young and good-looking.
We fell hopelessly in Love with each other.
We often played duets.

Our understanding was perfect.

But, of course, my parents very soon opposed
our union.

They destined me to a fiancé worthy of my rank.

So we ran away and married in a little chapel.

My parents sent men in search for us.

They found us and killed you.

I ended my life in a convent.

I never stopped loving you for one moment.

My death was very sweet.

At last I was going to find you again.

Today, again, I'm like a princess,
a princess rather deprived
waiting for her Prince Charming.
The prince is searching for a lost identity
and a fortune to offer to his lady;
once his rights are recognized,
he will come in search of his lady.
The princess believes that Love is sufficient unto
itself, and lives happy on feelings and fresh water.
The prince believes that Love cannot last
without fame and renown.
And in a world that knows no pity, he is right.
So, the princess waits, with patience, with languor.
And the prince offered her his hymn to Love
on a platter of gold and light.

I so often wonder why I returned to earth.
It's so hard for me to adapt to this world.
In fact, I know exactly what I have come to do but I
delayed my return for a long time, knowing if you
don't take care, life here is identical with suffering.

But I loved him so much
and still love him so much.
They killed him.
They took him from me.
They stopped me from loving him.
At last I was to come back and to live out my Love.
But I didn't come back to live in solitude
with happiness unshared.
This time Paul is truly there, he is alive.
He has his own independent fears

in addition to my existence.
All that is a lot for a man.

We must succeed; that's why I'm here.
It's my one objective.

During all my youth I had to fight to win my
liberty, to do what I wanted and most of all,
to love whom I chose.
My parents had to accept it, but I never gave way.
I had to assert myself fiercely.
Obviously I always fought alone.
My only strengths were a taste for the absolute
and a quest for the ideal whose form was still
unknown to me.
Nevertheless I was moving toward a familiar area.

But you are there, with your fears.
You're afraid of me, of my Love,
afraid of being pulled in, immersed.
Yes, I offer you total immersion as the best result.
A tide of Love which would carry us
further and further away.
Leap into the water.
Come and drink at the spring of my Love.
It will never dry up.
My Love will be your Love too.
For you that means prison, for me liberty.
Let our violins be in tune with each other.
Have faith in the other side that slumbers within you.

I discover, I advance; again I come up against
another interrogation.
How intriguing!
Never tiring, never tedious,
an eternal fountain of youth.
Whatever else shall I discover
that I don't already know?
At first I make out a few vague outlines.
I express crazy ideas and then one day I know.
I'm sad that I can't share these inspiring moments
of certainty with you.

You and I met at a very precise well-chosen time
of our existence.
Don't say, I beg you, that it was too early or too late.
It was exactly the right moment.
We had chosen this moment ourselves.
Before that I had to be reborn into my family with
my parents.
I had to live through several difficult childhood
years, and a love-life that I'd describe as an
apprenticeship — a kind of rehearsal, a draft.
It was all completely indispensable.
I had to go through all those stages in order to be
ready at last — ready to meet the person who was
going to turn my existence upside down.
You too had to learn and learn again.
We are all, without exception, in the same situation.

All these delays and complications which slow
down the life of our couple have a meaning.
We are not yet ready.
Will we be ready during this life?
The question's very interesting , don't you think?
There you are
with your uncertainties, your anxieties,
and the truths you conceal from yourself —
your contradictions and your lies.
Your greatest misfortune, perhaps, is your failure
to make your family respond to your
sensitive nature and your Love.

I'm not pursuing the Holy Grail, only Paul.

I often think of us as two phantoms,
two waves, or two psyches.
We are linked by a current of Love which does not
belong to the so-called real world.
My dearest wish is to give shape to this Love on
earth, a hope that gives me unbounded energy.
I'm not afraid of disappointment.
Would I have taken such a long journey to live
through an ordinary story?
In any case I hate colorless living,
living like everyone else.
There are endless ways of living a platonic Love,
endless ways of expressing one's feelings,
emotions, and sensuality.
Every form of art or writing brings people closer to
their deepest nature.

All means are good for avoiding a waste of energy
and maintain peace within oneself.
One can be very happy without descending
into the concrete world.
One can have a good life by staying in a world of
make-believe and dreams.
One can feel and respond without truly living
through material things, if only through the view-
point of imagination — a mixture of intelligent
concepts, memories, experiences, studies,
and earlier lives' recollection.
But I truly agree, we're on earth to try to achieve
total integration — earth and sky,
the imaginary and the real.

Once at a concert Paul played a short classical
introduction and someone in the audience murmured,
"It sounds like Chopin."
This remark made a strange impression on me.
After taking my first and only journey back into
my past life in Scotland,
I went to the library in order to locate
more precisely the period and the place.
I should say that I possess the gift of scanning
and finding the information I'm looking for
very quickly.
I tried to find out all I could about the
harpsichord and its precursor for I'm convinced
this instrument I played still exists
and is perhaps in a museum.
It was then, as I was studying a series of works

about the harpsichord and the piano, I came
across a photograph of Chopin's hand, reproduced
from a cast taken just after his death.
It was Paul's hand.
I thought I was going to faint.
I began searching again through all the
biographies of Chopin.
I was struck by the way he behaved
toward the first Love of his life.
His beloved said to him:
"You tell me you love me and the one thing you
do in a hurry is to leave me."
His best friend said about him:
"To marry while on the threshold of his career
would mean inflexibility and renunciation."
"He suffered desperately away from her,

but he needed that suffering."
Chopin said:
"I want to make a name for myself,
I want to earn money and then I'll come back."
"I'll come back provided I'd become rich enough
and famous enough to ask you to unite
your destiny with mine."
He left for Vienna and Berlin.
The lady waited for years, grew weary, and ended
by marrying a landowner by whom she had five
children.
At the age of thirty-five she became blind and
when receiving Chopin's faithful confidant, she
told him, her eyes brimming with tears,
that she had never stopped loving him.

I was very moved and upset by all these accounts.
One day a friend began to talk about Chopin and
the famous legend.
I was intrigued and asked him
to tell me more about it.
Apparently Chopin asked for his heart to be
removed after his death and buried in Poland
in the church of Saint Cross in Warsaw,
while his body would remain in France in the
cemetery of Père Lachaise in Paris.
I was very surprised for I thought I had read
everything about Chopin...
I went back to the library and consulted other
works in the archive room.
I found that this was true.
I wanted to photocopy the page relating this fact,

but I mistakenly chose the wrong page and
photographed another which was unconnected,
a gap of three hundred pages.
Then still following my intuition, I told myself
there had to be a good reason for my error.
And there was.
It was the only page in the book, of course
I checked it later, where the current name of
Paul's family occurs.

Later, and for the first time in my life (this life...)
I went to the Père Lachaise cemetery in Paris.
What an impression it made!
A magical, peaceful atmosphere; cats everywhere!
Most of the tombs are magnificent.
I was drawn to those

that were abandoned, lying open;
an ideal hiding-place for cats to have their kittens.
I felt particularly happy, transported into
another world.
Then came the shock.
Chopin's tomb is located in the 11th sector
and in pathway number 11.
Paul was born on the 11th.

Had Paul been Chopin or close to Chopin?
In any case I constantly receive signs from above
that are more than unusual.
All things are linked together.
From life to other lives we find ourselves again,
yet we have not succeeded in loving each other
in peace.

He was born on the 11th.
I was born on the 22nd.
He is half of me.
I am his double.

In numerology 11 and 22 are the two highest
numbers that cannot be reduced.

How firmly this man possesses me, how close he is
to me every second of my existence, like a spiritual
shadow; the few people to whom I can mention
this story believe it and sometimes even envy me.
I'm not lying, I'm living through this situation
with intensity — I'm carried along.
If these few friends follow me, are they influenced
by what I say, are they carried away by my sincerity?
I'm living out a tale of passionate Love,
a tale with no cloud, and a perpetual honeymoon...
My story causes astonishment, I'm transforming
nothingness into accomplishment.
But there cannot be smoke without fire, and the
brazier which makes me glow is vast.

I do not know a single united couple.
No doubt I know the wrong people
or else I'm too idealistic.
At one moment or another, there is always deceit,
lying, or hypocrisy on the part of one, and
submission, oppression, or domination on the other.
And couples can endure with much effort,
grief, and fear.
Where is the place for Love?
Love and shadows are mutually exclusive.
Love returned and shared goes perfectly with
facility and clarity.
My Love for you is very clear and simple.
Your Love for me cannot be complex.
That would be nonsense.
It would contradict the definition of the word Love.

Your Love for me hovers over you but you do not
want to see it open out in your life.
It is your most absolute right.
Only; do nothing to destroy that Love — keep it
on one side, that's all.
An attempt to destroy it would mean cutting the
soul away from yourself.
No Love is too big.
No Love is a burden on the soul.
The soul feeds on Love.
The soul needs Love
and all Love is good for the soul.
Accept this Love and this wild energy that are
destined for you, react to them, abuse them, and
forget that they come from me.
The realization of a union assumes a divine

character and should not be influenced or hurried.
In loving you I'm preparing a piece of ground to
receive you, but this will never happen if you do
not do the same thing.
Everything in the universe is sacred: a drop of rain,
an earthworm, or star dust.
Why have men forgotten it?
It's so pleasing to feel linked to everything.
Arrogance, pride, and vice belong only
to the kingdom of man.
I am not proud of belonging to the human race.
I feel much happier within nature and among
the animals; there I can be myself.
Yet I should like to shine for the man I love.
I just sank into oblivion.
There is no place for me in his world.

During your childhood
something very painful happened.
You lacked Love,
as though you had been abandoned.
You grew up in rigid, cold, and austere surroundings.
You were a child whose heart was ill-treated.
You were a youth whose feelings were disabled.
Sometimes I've imagined the worst in order
to explain your silences —
that you were suffering from a very serious illness
and you couldn't talk to me about it.
No doubt I would have done the same.
I would have said anything, I would have hidden
like an animal feeling its end approach.
Paul, don't leave before I do.

Wanting social success is quite legitimate, but
accepting concessions with oneself proves a great
lack of personality and shows no real wish
to know oneself.
When I talk like this I'm not passing judgment,
I'm not moralizing.
I'm trying to explain a behavior that I still don't
understand.
The man is complex and unyielding but I still
find him touching.

*"A man's true nature lies first of all in what he con-
ceals."*

André Malraux

A Love lived out intensively by one partner
and ignored by the other...
I don't believe it.
I harvest the fruits of my reflections
and I can't share them.
It's truly a pity and most of all very stupid.
I live through the present and I act here and now.
With you, everything is always postponed.
Years of total and sincere Love for nothing
leave me questioning, doubtful.
If I stop dreaming, I begin to feel unwell.
It's against my nature.
When I'm no longer in harmony I must dream
more and more.
I think I can persuade the angels on high that my
story is beautiful.

In return they send me many signs
encouraging me to continue.
Everyone believes in my story except him.
He has arranged his life in a way that proves
his sound egocentric nature.
When he has reached his goal, will he at last take
time to see himself as he really is; will he finally
converse with himself?
The major problem with men in search of social
recognition is that they are never really satisfied.
They pursue the unattainable goal;
always something more.

"Fame is the radiant mourning of happiness."
Madeleine Chapsal

When you try to persuade me that you're
worthless, that you don't deserve me,
what law have you in mind?
A universal law which would determine whether
people deserve each other or not?
Everything is deserved, my dear,
if one wants to have it.
There lies the problem.
Destiny can appear cruel.
Let us change our way of seeing.
If we stumble, if we encounter obstacles,
it's because we're not seeing clearly enough.

If you search without putting something of your
heart in it, you risk finding very little.

I should like to be no more than a wave,
a sweet music expressing warmth and energy,
a melody from the heart,
a timeless classic,
a comet, leaving a trail of light,
as the sandman who brings beautiful dreams.
To become a pure wave, moving at the speed of
light and beyond, moving across the world,
other worlds, the universe, other universes.
To travel in time and outside time.

We are all composed of vibrations,
more or less in harmony with each other.
The vibrations of our earthly body
are truly too slow.
There are worlds where those about to be married
exchange heart waves instead of wedding rings.
That's the world I'd like to return to with you.

We have seen each other rarely,
but very often the moon was full.
The moon is a planet that fascinates me.
Today the discoveries in astrophysics multiply and
our old romantic companion looks out of date.
Yet one only has to look up to observe her and she
offers a perpetually wonderful spectacle which
changes constantly.
When she plays with the sun,
then apotheosis occurs.

A few days after meeting you, I left for Madagascar,
called by the natives, Island of the Moon.
Then I brought back to you some photographs
taken there, my first and only setting of the moon
in a starry sky.

Then you dedicated pieces of music to me
entitled Madagaskar I and II.
So we offered the moon to each other.
Can one imagine a more beautiful element for sym-
bolizing a mystical and mysterious Love?

All that time we were both carefree.
You knew how to recreate that intense
emotion in music.
You were able to re-transmit that same emotion
while you agreed to follow the tide of your feelings.
Afterwards the freshness of these moments of
happiness flew away, you forgot me.
The mystery that I represented for you, a certain
source of inspiration, suddenly frightened you; you
no longer controlled your intellect sufficiently

and your demanding career claimed all your lucidity.
Strange for an artist.
But I was going to penetrate into a world that
belonged only to you — a world of inner struggles,
interminable and painful.
No doubt you wanted to keep me on one side
in order to protect me.
You refused my help and you didn't want to see
where my strength lay.
I've never been fragile, only extremely sensitive.

You know, I've got nothing to do with your ego,
your little superficial self, or your way of showing
off and appearing.
To my greatest delight, I fell in Love with your
deep being, your true essence, that part of you
which I surely perceive better than you do.
One day I grasped it and loved it, forever.
But you prefer to avoid your deep self for you
have the impression that it would prevent you
from succeeding in the aim you have fixed
for yourself.
If you became aware of this unity which dwells in
one's being, if you became aware that you are
always guided to reach the best aspect of yourself,
all your plans would be achieved rapidly and easily.
But you avoid listening to your heart.

You restrain your intuition and you exercise your
intellect to its maximum extent, remaining self-
satisfied within a fearsome and destructive cynicism.

I harass you with the intense bombardment of my
thoughts but you remain strangely hermetic.
You have forbidden yourself to feel me.
You have even made yourself incapable of writing
without your computer.
No doubt you're scared of revealing a few feelings
through your hands, for you know very well that
they cannot lie.
Dominate everything, organize everything, and
manage everything including your heart.
But you've got everything wrong.
You think you can master your feelings,

but you master nothing at all; you're repressing them.
That's a big deal.
I am not incarnate enough, you are too much so.

I have a profound need to communicate this unique
Love which is within me for I believe that deep with-
in us every human being seeks it and dreams about it.
Unfortunately our world today
leaves us little hope of finding it.
The world wants to be materialistic
more than anything else.
Feelings are put off until later, when we'll have time,
when we've been successful.
Love seems anachronistic

or belonging to another century.

But, in fact, everyone dreams of the absolute.

Most of the time people live with one being

and dream of another.

How horrible!

How sad!

One should not be content with what one has

if one is not satisfied.

One should search perpetually for the rare pearl.

The achievement of the ideal couple, perfect

harmony, and total osmosis is not a delusion.

The alchemy of the heart is not reserved for

initiates of the esoteric, it can be achieved by every

being who possesses a heart.

It is the only means of transmuting the body

toward a state of light, satisfaction, and permanency.

Everyone has a sister-soul somewhere within its
destiny and, in order to encounter it,
one must first of all believe it is possible.
The certainty of these ideas exists at the level of the
heart and if everyone dreams of it this is because it
belongs to the realm of the possible.
If one thinks that it can exist, one must not think
that it happens only to other people or only in novels.
Novelists invent nothing.
They go in search of fine romances
where they exist.
Nothing comes of nothing.
The brain is idiotic and it merely filters elements that
belong to other dimensions.
As far as I am concerned,
my story is absolutely authentic.

I live through all I write.
I do not write to convince others.
I only want people to realize that the ideal
I describe is not a fantasy.
It exists within each one of us.
It is for each one of us to feel it and want it very
deeply in order to lay its foundations, for it needs
work in real depth and work that is
profoundly personal.
It is no use behaving like other people and
following the other sheep.
Each one of us must bring our true self into it.

Being a couple does not mean
losing one's personality.
Most of the time, it's true, there is always one
partner who loses, one who is stifled.
A true exchange can be established to allow the
two beings to affirm themselves without losing
their plumage or assuming an unhealthy power.
To give Love is to permit the other person to grow
and blossom for his or her greatest pleasure.
Man and woman,
two solitudes who protect and complete the other.
By transforming one's gaze, one's vision of the
world, one is able to change that world.

If my Love exists, if your Love exists,
then everything is possible.
The worst, we live through it apart,
let us live the best together.
Life is only a vast play, is that not so?
A character acts her joys and sorrows.
If we refuse to act, we die.
If we refuse to love,
we ruin our life and pass what is essential.

I feel I've known you since the beginning of time.
I signed a Love pact with you the day I met you.
I didn't know you could forget it.
I must try to accept your choice.
You know too what you're doing in making that
decision.
I don't hold the key to your life
in the name of Love.
But I didn't sign this pact of my own.
At the dawn of creation, at the moment when we
separated, so that we could each live even more
freely, you too knew that we would be
linked for eternity.
No doubt you're more keen on liberty than I am
and you've many more things to live through
than I have.

As our lives passed we've evolved in different
ways and we haven't oriented our inner researches
in the same way.
I want to hurry things along and maybe I'm mis-
taken, but perhaps, too, it's the right moment to
make you act, perhaps it's the right moment for us
to come together again?
You know very well I don't act in any
thoughtless way.
I'm not out of my mind and I'm not nuts.
I've tried for years to remain as discreet as possible.
I thought you needed to be far away from me in
order to resolve your personal problems.
And I thought this solitude was beneficial
for me as well.
I should have died of grief thousands of times over.

But now, that's enough.
I must move to a more concrete,
a more terrestrial dimension.
I'm a woman made of flesh and blood and I want
my body and mind to feel the thrills of life.
To be capable of sublimating and transcending
everything is great.
I'm lucky enough to possess this strength,
but now I want something else.
I want everything.

I constantly receive messages from above.
I request and obtain replies;
and it happens more and more easily.
It's as though I had understood the trick.
I succeed in making the connection

and sometimes I have the impression that
the situation is permanent.
How many times have I really tried to forget you?
And each time a disturbing coincidence occurred.
So, I've made the firm resolution that I won't try
any longer to forget you, I'll concentrate on you.
The results are even more coincidences.
In the end I have become my own clairvoyant.

> *"The heart has a computing ability that is far*
> *more accurate and far more precise than any-*
> *thing within the limits of rational thought."*
> *Deepak Chopra - The Seven*
> *Spiritual Laws of Success*

My unconscious knows where to look
for information.
Has it any motive for lying to me,
directing me the wrong way?
Most of all, doesn't it wish me well?

I'm guided toward Paul.

The signs are given in order to help,
not to lead me astray.
My inner voice guides my way
and there is no rational explanation.
There are no directions for use when you
encounter the other world.
There are only close convictions,
sensations, and revelations.

I don't know if I could be happy sharing your life
today, but I could never have been happy with you
at the time we met.
I had personal problems to solve and although
nothing is completely settled,
I love you more now.
Loving cannot be reduced to living
the life of a couple.
I could have been very happy looking after you,
making your daily life easier and
remaining in your shadow.
From that point of view my ego
gives me no problems.

The main thing is to be happy.

There are a thousand ways of being happy.
But it would have been a pity if I could not have
developed as an individual as I could have done
without you.
I've succeeded in being in good shape without
you, but you have always been present in my
everyday life, in my deep meditations as in all my
mundane activities.
Perhaps I should found a school?
"Find happiness: Love in solitude —
available to all"...
I can well imagine the burden it can be for you,
the simple fact of my saying that you live in me,
that you are within me.
You know that I only project positive thoughts
in your direction.

The thing that seems negative to you is the fact
that I am transmitting them.
But in spite of everything, and in spite of you,
I shall always be there trying to protect you
whenever I feel you're in danger.
I was born for this purpose.
It is as though you were me —
the instinct for self-preservation.
That is vital.
Separating from you would be the death of me and I
do not want to die.
I have enough life for two people.
One day I told you rather lightheartedly that
I loved you as much as if I were two people.
I didn't realize I was saying something so true.

I have so much need for peace and quiet at the
moment that I no longer know whether I could
face up to your fitful and shocking bad moods.
But, I'm a starter all the same.
A challenge for Love.

For in the end, perhaps, I don't love you at all,
little prince.

I hate your world with life managed, organized,
and lived out by telephone.
Most of all I hate the talk that says nothing,
filling the void with nothing.
Today people cultivate one's mind and react
through the medium of computers.
I like modernity in tranquillity, comfort in lucidity.

I don't like letting myself be overtaken by any
system and not remaining totally in control
of what I do.

In fact, you are not free and that breaks my heart
for you are very gifted and you would be com-
pletely liberated and serene if you heeded your
intuition instead of satisfying your ego and
depending on the goodwill of others.

Your path is not called Helena, it is called you.

Is such a Love conceivable in the real world?

Could a life together be possible?
Would ordinary life allow us to devote ourselves
to each other body and soul
without the slightest shadow?
Could our two egos exchange a show of affection
without a hint of selfishness?
Both of us have access to an unusual degree of
sensitivity, we make our way into magical
creative worlds,
but we must remain perpetually vigilant.
This universe and its marvels can, in one fraction
of a second, become a veritable desert.
The desert of the mind.
We all struggle to achieve our dreams.

The struggle is more or less noble.
It is only a question of value.
I dream, you dream, we dream.
We come together in our night-time dreams
and I remain alone in my dreams by day.
All through my days I think about our nights
while you spend your days forgetting our nights.
It is most important to dream.
If your night-time lady has another name, be
careful if she is not called Love.

Dream, dream my Love and offer yourself eternity.

Anyone wishing to write to
Helena Weiss-Meyer
may do so at the following address:

P.O. Box 642262
San Francisco
CA 94164-2262